let's cook

chocolate

Jacqueline
Bellefontaine

p

Contents

Family Chocolate Cake

A simple to make family cake ideal for an everyday treat. Keep the decoration
as simple as you like – you could use a bought icing or filling, if liked.

Serves 8-10

INGREDIENTS

125 g/4¹/2 oz/¹/2 cup soft margarine
125 g/4¹/2 oz/¹/2 cup caster
   (superfine) sugar
2 eggs
1 tbsp golden (light corn) syrup
125 g/4¹/2 oz/1 cup self-raising flour,
   sieved (strained)

2 tbsp cocoa powder, sieved
   (strained)

FILLING AND TOPPING:
50 g/1³/4 oz/¹/4 cup icing
   (confectioners') sugar, sieved
   (strained)

25 g/1 oz/2 tbsp butter
100 g/3¹/2 oz white or milk cooking
   chocolate
a little milk or white chocolate,
   melted (optional)

1 Lightly grease two 18 cm/7 inch shallow cake tins (pans).

2 Place all of the ingredients for the cake in a large mixing bowl and beat with a wooden spoon or electric hand whisk to form a smooth mixture.

3 Divide the mixture between the prepared tins (pans) and level the tops. Bake in a preheated oven, 190°C/325°F/Gas Mark 5, for 20 minutes or until springy to the touch. Cool for a few minutes in the tins (pans) before transferring to a wire rack to cool completely.

4 To make the filling, beat the icing (confectioners') sugar and butter together in a bowl until light and fluffy. Melt the cooking chocolate and beat half into the icing mixture. Use the filling to sandwich the 2 cakes together.

5 Spread the remaining melted cooking chocolate over the top of the cake. Pipe circles of contrasting melted milk or white chocolate and feather into the cooking chocolate with a cocktail stick (toothpick), if liked. Leave to set before serving.

COOK'S TIP

Ensure that you eat this cake on the day of baking, as it does not keep well.

Mocha Layer Cake

*Chocolate cake and a creamy coffee-flavoured filling
are combined in this delicious mocha cake.*

Serves 8-10

INGREDIENTS

200 g/7³/₄ oz/1 cup self-raising flour
¹/₄ tsp baking powder
4 tbsp cocoa powder
100 g/3¹/₂ oz/7 tbsp caster
  (superfine) sugar
2 eggs
2 tbsp golden (light corn) syrup

150 ml/¹/₄ pint/²/₃ cup sunflower oil
150 ml/¹/₄ pint/²/₃ cup milk

FILLING:
1 tsp instant coffee
1 tbsp boiling water
300 ml/¹/₂ pint/1¹/₄ cups double
  (heavy) cream

25 g/1 oz/2 tbsp icing
  (confectioners') sugar

TO DECORATE:
50 g/1³/₄ oz flock chocolate
chocolate caraque
icing (confectioners') sugar, to dust

1 Lightly grease three 18 cm/
7 inch cake tins (pans).

2 Sieve (strain) the flour,
baking powder and cocoa
powder into a large mixing bowl.
Stir in the sugar. Make a well in
the centre and stir in the eggs,
syrup, oil and milk. Beat with a
wooden spoon, gradually mixing
in the dry ingredients to make a
smooth batter. Divide the mixture
between the prepared tins (pans).

3 Bake in a preheated oven,
180°C/350°F/Gas Mark 4, for
35-45 minutes or until springy to
the touch. Leave in the tins (pans)
for 5 minutes, then turn out on to
a wire rack to cool completely.

4 Dissolve the instant coffee in
the boiling water and place in
a bowl with the cream and icing
(confectioners') sugar. Whip until
the cream is just holding it's shape.
Use half of the cream to sandwich

the 3 cakes together. Spread the
remaining cream over the top and
sides of the cake. Lightly press the
flock chocolate into the cream
around the edge of the cake.

5 Transfer to a serving plate. Lay
the caraque over the top of
the cake. Cut a few thin strips of
baking parchment and place on top
of the caraque. Dust lightly with
icing (confectioners') sugar, then
carefully remove the paper. Serve.

Rich Chocolate Layer Cake

*Thin layers of delicious light chocolate cake sandwiched
together with a rich chocolate icing.*

Serves 10–12

INGREDIENTS

7 eggs
200 g/7 oz/1³/₄ cups caster
   (superfine) sugar
150 g/5¹/₂ oz/1¹/₄ cups plain (all-
   purpose) flour
50 g/1³/₄ oz/¹/₂ cup cocoa powder
50 g/1³/₄ oz/4 tbsp butter, melted

FILLING:
200 g/7 oz dark chocolate
125 g/4¹/₂ oz/¹/₂ cup butter
50 g/1³/₄ oz/4 tbsp icing
   (confectioners') sugar

TO DECORATE:
75 g/2³/₄ oz/10 tbsp toasted flaked
   almonds, crushed lightly
small chocolate curls
   or grated chocolate

1 Grease a deep 23 cm/9 inch square cake tin (pan) and line the base with baking parchment.

2 Whisk the eggs and caster (superfine) sugar in a mixing bowl with an electric whisk for about 10 minutes, or until the mixture is very light and foamy and the whisk leaves a trail that lasts a few seconds when lifted.

3 Sieve (strain) the flour and cocoa together and fold half into the mixture. Drizzle over the melted butter and fold in the rest of the flour and cocoa. Pour into the prepared tin (pan) and bake in a preheated oven, 180°C/350°F/ Gas Mark 4, for 30-35 minutes or until springy to the touch. Leave to cool slightly, then remove from the tin (pan) and cool completely on a wire rack. Wash and dry the tin (pan) and return the cake to it.

4 To make the filling, melt the chocolate and butter together, then remove from the heat. Stir in the icing (confectioners') sugar, leave to cool, then beat until thick enough to spread.

5 Halve the cake lengthways and cut each half into 3 layers. Sandwich the layers together with three-quarters of the chocolate filling. Spread the remainder over the cake and mark a wavy pattern on the top. Press the almonds on to the sides. Decorate with chocolate curls or grated chocolate.

Chocolate Passion Cake

What could be nicer than passion cake with added chocolate?
Rich and moist, this cake is fabulous with afternoon tea.

Serves 10–12

INGREDIENTS

5 eggs
150 g/5^1/$_2$ oz/^{2}/$_3$ cup caster (superfine) sugar
150 g/5^1/$_2$ oz/1^1/$_4$ cups plain (all-purpose) flour

40 g/1^1/$_2$ oz/^{1}/$_3$ cup cocoa powder
175 g/6 oz carrots, peeled, finely grated and squeezed until dry
50 g/1^3/$_4$ oz/^{1}/$_2$ cup chopped walnuts
2 tbsp sunflower oil

350 g/12 oz medium fat soft cheese
175 g/6 oz/1 cup icing (confectioners') sugar
175 g/6 oz milk or dark chocolate, melted

1 Lightly grease and line the base of a 20 cm/8 inch deep round cake tin (pan).

2 Place the eggs and sugar in a large mixing bowl set over a pan of gently simmering water and whisk until very thick. Lift the whisk up and let the mixture drizzle back – it will leave a trail for a few seconds when thick enough.

3 Remove the bowl from the heat. Sieve (strain) the flour and cocoa powder into the bowl and carefully fold in. Fold in the carrots, walnuts and oil until just combined.

4 Pour into the prepared tin (pan) and bake in a preheated oven, 190°C/375°F/Gas Mark 5, for 45 minutes. Leave to cool slightly then turn out on to a wire rack to cool completely.

5 Beat together the soft cheese and icing (confectioners') sugar until combined. Beat in the melted chocolate. Split the cake in half and sandwich together again with half of the chocolate mixture. Cover the top of the cake with the remainder of the chocolate mixture, swirling it with a knife. Leave to chill or serve at once.

COOK'S TIP

The undecorated cake can be frozen for up to 2 months. Defrost at room temperature for 3 hours or overnight in the refrigerator.

Chocolate Truffle Cake

Soft chocolatey sponge topped with a rich chocolate truffle mixture
makes a cake that chocoholics will die for.

Serves 12

INGREDIENTS

75 g/2³/4 oz/¹/3 cup butter
75 g/2³/4 oz/¹/3 cup caster
   (superfine) sugar
2 eggs, lightly beaten
75 g/2³/4 oz/²/3 cup self-raising flour
¹/2 tsp baking powder
25 g/1 oz/¹/4 cup cocoa powder
50 g/1³/4 oz ground almonds

TRUFFLE TOPPING:
350 g/12 oz dark chocolate
100 g/3¹/2 oz butter
300 ml/¹/2 pint/1¹/4 cups double
   (heavy) cream
75 g/2³/4 oz/1¹/4 cups plain cake
   crumbs
3 tbsp dark rum

TO DECORATE:
Cape gooseberries
50 g/1³/4 oz dark chocolate, melted

1 Lightly grease a 20 cm/8 inch round springform tin (pan) and line the base. Beat together the butter and sugar until light and fluffy. Gradually add the eggs, beating well after each addition.

2 Sieve (strain) the flour, baking powder and cocoa powder together and fold into the mixture along with the ground almonds. Pour into the prepared tin (pan) and bake in a preheated oven, 180°C/350°F/Gas Mark 4, for 20-25 minutes or until springy to the touch. Leave to cool slightly in the tin (pan), then transfer to a wire rack to cool completely. Wash and dry the tin (pan) and return the cooled cake to the tin (pan).

3 To make the topping, heat the chocolate, butter and cream in a heavy-based pan over a low heat and stir until smooth. Cool, then chill for 30 minutes. Beat well with a wooden spoon and chill for a further 30 minutes. Beat the mixture again, then add the cake crumbs and rum, beating until well combined. Spoon over the sponge base and chill for 3 hours.

4 Meanwhile, dip the Cape gooseberries in the melted chocolate until partially covered. Leave to set on baking parchment. Transfer the cake to a serving plate; decorate with Cape gooseberries.

No Bake Chocolate Squares

These are handy little squares to keep in the refrigerator for when unexpected guests arrive. Children will enjoy making these as an introduction to chocolate cookery.

Makes 16

INGREDIENTS

275 g/9^1/$_2$ oz dark chocolate
175 g/6 oz/^{3}/$_4$ cup butter
4 tbsp golden (light corn) syrup
2 tbsp dark rum (optional)

175 g/6 oz plain biscuits (cookies),
  such as Rich Tea
25 g/1 oz toasted rice cereal
50 g/1^3/$_4$ oz/^{1}/$_2$ cup chopped walnuts
  or pecan nuts

100 g/3^1/$_2$ oz/^{1}/$_2$ cup glacé (candied)
  cherries, chopped roughly
25 g/1 oz white chocolate, to
  decorate

1 Place the dark chocolate in a large mixing bowl with the butter, syrup and rum, if using, and set over a saucepan of gently simmering water until melted, stirring until blended.

2 Break the biscuits (cookies) into small pieces and stir into the chocolate mixture along with the rice cereal, nuts and cherries.

3 Line an 18 cm/7inch square cake tin (pan) with baking parchment. Pour the mixture into the tin (pan) and level the top,

pressing down well with the back of a spoon. Chill for 2 hours.

4 To decorate, melt the white chocolate and drizzle it over the top of the cake in a random pattern. Leave to set. To serve, carefully turn out of the tin (pan) and remove the baking parchment. Cut into 16 squares.

COOK'S TIP

Store in an airtight container in the refrigerator for up to 2 weeks.

VARIATION

Brandy or an orange-flavoured liqueur can be used instead of the rum, if you prefer. Cherry brandy also works well.

VARIATION

For a coconut flavour, replace the rice cereal with desiccated (shredded) coconut and add a coconut-flavoured liqueur.

Sticky Chocolate Brownies

*Everyone loves chocolate brownies and these are so gooey
and delicious they are impossible to resist!*

Makes 9

INGREDIENTS

100 g/3^{1}/$_2$ oz/generous ^{1}/$_3$ cup
  unsalted butter
175 g/6 oz/^{3}/$_4$ cup caster (superfine)
  sugar
75 g/2 ^{3}/$_4$ oz/^{1}/$_2$ cup dark muscovado
  sugar

125 g/4^1/$_2$ oz dark chocolate
1 tbsp golden (light corn) syrup
2 eggs
1 tsp chocolate or vanilla flavouring
  (extract)

100 g/3^1/$_2$ oz/^{3}/$_4$ cup plain (all-
  purpose) flour
2 tbsp cocoa powder
^{1}/$_2$ tsp baking powder

1 Lightly grease a 20 cm/8 inch shallow square cake tin (pan) and line the base.

2 Place the butter, sugars, dark chocolate and golden (light corn) syrup in a heavy-based saucepan and heat gently, stirring until the mixture is well blended and smooth. Remove from the heat and leave to cool.

3 Beat together the eggs and flavouring (extract). Whisk in the cooled chocolate mixture.

4 Sieve (strain) together the flour, cocoa powder and baking powder and fold carefully into the egg and chocolate mixture, using a metal spoon or a spatula.

5 Spoon the mixture into the prepared tin (pan) and bake in a preheated oven, 180°C/350°F/ Gas Mark 4, for 25 minutes until the top is crisp and the edge of the cake is beginning to shrink away from the tin (pan). The inside of the cake mixture will still be quite stodgy and soft to the touch.

6 Leave the cake to cool completely in the tin (pan), then cut it into squares to serve.

COOK'S TIP

*This cake can be well wrapped
and frozen for up to 2 months.
Defrost at room temperature for
about 2 hours or overnight in
the refrigerator.*

Chocolate Chip Muffins

Muffins are always popular and are so simple to make. I make mini muffins for my young children which are fabulous bite-size treats or perfect for children parties.

Makes 12

INGREDIENTS

100 g/3¹/₂ oz/generous ¹/₃ cup soft margarine

225 g/8 oz/1 cup caster (superfine) sugar

2 large eggs

150 ml/¹/₄ pint/²/₃ cup whole milk natural yogurt

5 tbsp milk

275 g/9¹/₂ oz/2 cups plain (all-purpose) flour

1 tsp bicarbonate of soda (baking soda)

175 g/6 oz dark chocolate chips

1 Line 12 muffin tins (pans) with paper cases.

2 Place the margarine and sugar in a large mixing bowl and beat with a wooden spoon until light and fluffy. Beat in the eggs, yogurt and milk until combined.

3 Sieve (strain) the flour and bicarbonate of soda (baking soda) together and add to the mixture. Stir until just blended.

4 Stir in the chocolate chips, then spoon the mixture into the paper cases and bake in a preheated oven, 190°C/375°F/Gas Mark 5, for 25 minutes or until a fine skewer inserted into the centre comes out clean. Leave to cool in the tin (pan) for 5 minutes, then turn out on to a wire rack to cool completely.

VARIATION

The mixture can also be used to make 6 large or 24 mini muffins. Bake mini muffins for 10 minutes or until springy to the touch.

VARIATION

For chocolate and orange muffins, add the grated rind of 1 orange and replace the milk with fresh orange juice.

Chocolate Eclairs

*Patisserie cream is the traditional filling for éclairs, but if time
is short you can fill them with whipped cream.*

Makes about 10

INGREDIENTS

CHOUX PASTRY (PIE DOUGH):
150 ml/^{1}/4 pint/^{2}/3 cup water
60 g/2 oz/^{1}/4 cup butter, cut into
  small pieces
90 g/3 oz/^{3}/4 cup strong plain (all-
  purpose) flour, sieved (strained)
2 eggs

PATISSERIE CREAM:
2 eggs, lightly beaten
50 g/1^3/4 oz/4 tbsp caster (superfine)
  sugar
2 tbsp cornflour (cornstarch)
300 ml/^{1}/2 pint/1^1/4 cups milk
^{1}/4 tsp vanilla flavouring (extract)

ICING:
25 g/1 oz/2 tbsp butter
1 tbsp milk
1 tbsp cocoa powder
100 g/3^1/2 oz/^{1}/2 cup icing
  (confectioners') sugar
a little white chocolate, melted

1 Lightly grease a baking tray (cookie sheet). Place the water in a saucepan, add the butter and heat gently until the butter melts. Bring to a rolling boil, then remove the pan from the heat and add the flour in one go, beating well until the mixture leaves the sides of the pan and forms a ball. Leave to cool slightly, then gradually beat in the eggs to form a smooth, glossy mixture. Spoon into a large piping bag fitted with a 1 cm/^{1}/2 inch plain nozzle (tip).

2 Sprinkle the tray (sheet) with a little water. Pipe éclairs 7.5 cm/ 3 inches long, spaced well apart. Bake in a preheated oven, 200°C/ 400°F/Gas Mark 6, for 30-35 minutes or until crisp and golden. Make a small slit in each one to let the steam escape; cool on a rack.

3 To make the patisserie cream, whisk the eggs and sugar until thick and creamy, then fold in the cornflour (cornstarch). Heat the milk until almost boiling and pour on to the eggs, whisking. Transfer to the pan and cook over a low heat, stirring until thick. Remove the pan from the heat and stir in the flavouring (extract). Cover with baking parchment and cool. To make the icing, melt the butter with the milk in a pan, remove from the heat and stir in the cocoa and sugar. Split the éclairs lengthways and pipe in the patisserie cream. Spread the icing over the top of the éclair. Spoon over the white chocolate, swirl in and leave to set.

Chocolate Crispy Bites

A favourite with children, this version of crispy bites have been given a new twist which is sure to be popular.

Makes 16

INGREDIENTS

WHITE LAYER:
50 g/1³/4 oz/4 tbsp butter
1 tbsp golden (light corn) syrup
150 g/5¹/2 oz white chocolate

50 g/1³/4 oz toasted rice cereal

DARK LAYER:
50 g/1³/4 oz/4 tbsp butter
2 tbsp golden (light corn) syrup

125 g/dark chocolate, broken into
   small pieces
75 g/2³/4 oz toasted rice cereal

1 Grease a 20 cm/8 inch square cake tin (pan) and line with baking parchment.

2 To make the white chocolate layer, melt the butter, golden (light corn) syrup and chocolate in a bowl set over a saucepan of gently simmering water.

3 Remove from the heat and stir in the rice cereal until it is well combined .

4 Press into the prepared tin (pan) and level the surface.

5 To make the dark chocolate layer, melt the butter, golden (light corn) syrup and dark chocolate in a bowl set over a pan of gently simmering water.

6 Remove from the heat and stir in the rice cereal until it is well coated. Pour the dark chocolate layer over the hardened white chocolate layer and chill until the top layer has hardened.

7 Turn out of the cake tin (pan) and cut into small squares, using a sharp knife.

COOK'S TIP

These bites can be made up to 4 days ahead. Keep them covered in the refrigerator until ready to use.

Chocolate Chip Cookies

No chocolate cook's repertoire would be complete without a chocolate chip cookie recipe.
This is sure to be a favourite as the basic recipe can be used to make several variations.

Makes about 18

INGREDIENTS

175 g/6 oz/1^1/$_2$ cups plain (all-purpose) flour
1 tsp baking powder
125 g/4^1/$_2$ oz/^{1}/$_2$ cup soft margarine

90 g/3 oz/generous ^{1}/$_2$ cup light muscovado sugar
60 g/2 oz/^{1}/$_4$ cup caster (superfine) sugar

^{1}/$_2$ tsp vanilla flavouring (extract)
1 egg
125 g/4^1/$_2$ oz/^{2}/$_3$ cup dark chocolate chips

1 Lightly grease 2 baking trays (cookie sheets).

2 Place all of the ingredients in a large mixing bowl and beat until well combined.

3 Place tablespoonfuls of the mixture on to the baking trays (cookie sheets), spacing them well apart to allow for spreading during cooking.

4 Bake in a preheated oven, 190°C/375°F/Gas Mark 5, for 10-12 minutes or until the cookies are golden brown.

5 Using a palette knife (spatula), transfer the cookies to a wire rack to cool completely.

VARIATIONS

For Choc & Nut Cookies, add 40 g/1^1/$_2$ oz/^{1}/$_4$ cup chopped hazelnuts to the basic mixture.

For Double Choc Cookies, beat in 40 g/1^1/$_2$ oz melted dark chocolate.

For White Chocolate Chip Cookies, use white chocolate chips instead of the dark chocolate chips.

VARIATIONS

For Mixed Chocolate Chip Cookies, use a mixture of dark, milk and white chocolate chips in the basic mixture.

For Chocolate Chip & Coconut Cookies, add 25 g/1 oz/^{1}/$_3$ cup desiccated (shredded) coconut to the basic mixture.

For Chocolate Chip & Raisin Cookies, add 40 g/1^1/$_2$ oz/ 5 tbsp raisins to the basic mixture.

Chocolate Fudge Pudding

This fabulous steamed pudding, served with a rich chocolate fudge sauce, is perfect for cold winter days – and it can be made in double quick time in the microwave, if you have one.

Serves 6

INGREDIENTS

150 g/5^1/2 oz/generous ^{1}/3 cup soft
margarine
150 g/5^1/2 oz/1^1/4 cups self-raising
flour
150 g/5^1/2 oz/^{1}/2 cup golden (light
corn) syrup

3 eggs
25 g/1 oz/^{1}/4 cup cocoa powder

CHOCOLATE FUDGE SAUCE:
100 g/3^1/2 oz dark chocolate
125 ml/4 fl oz/^{1}/2 cup sweetened
condensed milk
4 tbsp double (heavy) cream

1 Lightly grease a 1.2 litre/
2 pint/5 cup pudding basin.

2 Place the ingredients for
the sponge in a mixing
bowl and beat until well
combined and smooth.

3 Spoon into the prepared
basin and level the top. Cover
with a disc of baking parchment
and tie a pleated sheet of foil over
the basin. Steam for 1^1/2-2 hours
until the pudding is cooked and
springy to the touch.

4 To make the sauce, break the
chocolate into small pieces
and place in a small pan with the
condensed milk. Heat gently,
stirring until the chocolate melts.

5 Remove the pan from the
heat and stir in the double
(heavy) cream.

6 To serve the pudding, turn it
out on to a serving plate and
pour over a little of the chocolate
fudge sauce. Serve the remaining
sauce separately.

COOK'S TIP

*To cook the cake in the microwave,
cook it, uncovered, on High for
4 minutes, turning the basin once.
Leave to stand for at least 5
minutes before turning out. Whilst
the pudding is standing, make the
sauce. Break the chocolate into
pieces and place in a microwave-
proof bowl with the milk. Cook on
High for 1 minute, then stir until
the chocolate melts. Stir in the
double (heavy) cream and serve.*

Saucy Chocolate Pudding

In this recipe, the mixture separates out during cooking to produce a cream sponge topping and a delicious chocolate sauce on the bottom.

Serves 4

INGREDIENTS

300 ml/$^1/_2$ pint/1$^1/_4$ cups milk
75 g/2$^3/_4$ oz dark chocolate
$^1/_2$ tsp vanilla flavouring (extract)
100 g/3$^1/_2$ oz/7 tbsp caster
   (superfine) sugar
100 g/3$^1/_2$ oz/generous $^1/_3$ cup butter

150 g/5$^1/_2$ oz/1$^1/_4$ cups self-raising
   flour
2 tbsp cocoa powder
icing (confectioners') sugar, to dust

FOR THE SAUCE:
3 tbsp cocoa powder
50 g/1$^3/_4$ oz/4 tbsp light muscovado
   sugar
300 ml/$^1/_2$ pint/1$^1/_4$ cups boiling
   water

1 Lightly grease an 850 ml\1$^1/_2$ pint/3$^3/_4$ cup ovenproof dish.

2 Place the milk in a small pan. Break the chocolate into pieces and add to the milk. Heat gently, stirring until the chocolate melts. Leave to cool slightly. Stir in the vanilla flavouring (extract).

3 Beat together the caster (superfine) sugar and butter in a bowl until light and fluffy. Sieve (strain) the flour and cocoa powder together. Add to the bowl with the chocolate milk and beat until smooth, using an electric whisk if you have one. Pour the mixture into the prepared dish.

4 To make the sauce, mix together the cocoa powder and sugar. Add a little boiling water and mix to a smooth paste, then stir in the remaining water. Pour the sauce over the pudding but do not mix in.

5 Place the dish on to a baking tray (cookie sheet) and bake in a preheated oven, 180°C/350°F/ Gas Mark 4, for 40 minutes or until dry on top and springy to the touch. Leave to stand for about 5 minutes, then dust with a little icing (confectioners') sugar just before serving.

VARIATION

For a mocha sauce, add 1 tbsp instant coffee to the cocoa powder and sugar in step 4, before mixing to a paste with the boiling water.

Chocolate Fondue

This is a fun dessert to serve at the end of the meal. Prepare
in advance, then just warm through before serving.

Serves 6–8

INGREDIENTS

CHOCOLATE FONDUE:
225 g/8 oz dark chocolate

200 ml/7 fl oz/^{3}/$_4$ cup double (heavy)
cream
2 tbsp brandy

TO SERVE:
selection of fruit
white and pink marshmallows
sweet biscuits (cookies)

1 Break the chocolate into small pieces and place in a small saucepan with the double (heavy) cream.

2 Heat the mixture gently, stirring constantly until the chocolate has melted and blended with the cream.

3 Remove the pan from the heat and stir in the brandy.

4 Pour into a fondue pot or a small flameproof dish and keep warm, preferably over a small burner.

5 Serve with a selection of fruit, marshmallows and biscuits (cookies) for dipping. The fruit and marshmallows can be spiked on fondue forks, wooden skewers or ordinary forks for dipping into the chocolate fondue.

COOK'S TIP

To prepare the fruit for dipping, cut larger fruit into bite-size pieces. Fruit which discolours, such as bananas, apples and pears, should be dipped in a little lemon juice as soon as it is cut.

COOK'S TIP

It is not essential to use a special fondue set. Dish warmers which use a night light are just as good for keeping the fondue warm. If you do not have one, stand the fondue dish in a larger dish and pour in enough boiling water to come halfway up the fondue dish. Whichever method you use to keep your fondue warm, place it on a heatproof stand to protect the table.

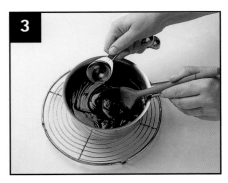

Chocolate Mint Swirl

*The classic combination of chocolate and mint flavours makes
an attractive dessert for special occasions.*

Serves 6

INGREDIENTS

300 ml/^{1}/2 pint/1^1/4 cups double
(heavy) cream
150 ml/^{1}/4 pint/^{2}/3 cup creamy
fromage frais

25 g/1 oz/2 tbsp icing (confectioners')
sugar
1 tbsp crème de menthe
175 g/6 oz dark chocolate

chocolate, to decorate

1 Place the cream in a large mixing bowl and whisk until standing in soft peaks.

2 Fold in the fromage frais and icing (confectioners') sugar, then place about one-third of the mixture in a smaller bowl. Stir the crème de menthe into the smaller bowl. Melt the dark chocolate and stir it into the remaining mixture.

3 Place alternate spoonfuls of the 2 mixtures into serving glasses, then swirl the mixture together to give a decorative effect. Leave to chill until required.

4 To make the piped chocolate decorations, melt a small amount of chocolate and place in a paper piping bag.

5 Place a sheet of baking parchment on a board and pipe squiggles, stars or flower shapes with the melted chocolate. Alternatively, to make curved decorations, pipe decorations on to a long strip of baking parchment, then carefully place the strip over a rolling pin, securing with sticky tape. Leave the chocolate to set, then carefully remove from the baking parchment.

6 Decorate each dessert with piped chocolate decorations and serve. The desserts can be decorated and then chilled, if preferred.

COOK'S TIP

*Pipe the patterns freehand or draw
patterns on to baking parchment
first, turn the parchment over
and then pipe the chocolate,
following the drawn outline.*

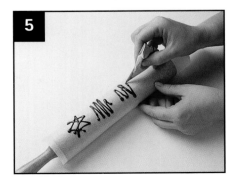

Chocolate Hazelnut Pots

Chocoholics will adore these creamy desserts consisting of a rich baked chocolate custard with the delicious flavour of hazelnuts.

Serves 6

INGREDIENTS

2 eggs
2 egg yolks
15 g/^{1}/$_2$ oz/1 tbsp caster (superfine) sugar

1 tsp cornflour (cornstarch)
600 ml/1 pint/2^1/$_2$ cups milk
75 g/3 oz dark chocolate
4 tbsp chocolate and hazelnut spread

TO DECORATE:
grated chocolate or large chocolate curls

1 Beat together the eggs, egg yolks, caster (superfine) sugar and cornflour (cornstarch) until well combined. Heat the milk until almost boiling.

2 Gradually pour the milk on to the eggs, whisking as you do so. Melt the chocolate and hazelnut spread in a bowl set over a pan of gently simmering water, then whisk the melted chocolate mixture into the eggs.

3 Pour into 6 small ovenproof dishes and cover the dishes with foil. Place them in a roasting tin (pan). Fill the tin (pan) with boiling water to come halfway up the sides of the dishes.

4 Bake in a preheated oven, 170°C/325°F/Gas Mark 3, for 35-40 minutes until the custard is just set. Remove from the tin (pan) and cool, then chill until required. Serve decorated with grated chocolate or chocolate curls.

COOK'S TIP

The foil lid prevents a skin forming on the surface of the custards.

COOK'S TIP

This dish is traditionally made in little pots called pots de crème, *which are individual ovenproof dishes with a lid. Ramekins (custard pots) are fine. The dessert can also be made in one large dish; cook for about 1 hour or until set.*

Chocolate Marquise

This is a classic French dish, part way between a mousse and parfait. It is usually chilled in a large mould (mold), but here it is served in individual moulds (molds).

Serves 6

INGREDIENTS

200 g/7 oz dark chocolate
100 g/3 1/2 oz/generous 1/3 cup butter
3 egg yolks
75 g/2 3/4 oz/1/3 cup caster (superfine) sugar

1 tsp chocolate flavouring (extract) or 1 tbsp chocolate-flavoured liqueur
300 ml/1/2 pint/1 1/4 cups double (heavy) cream

TO SERVE:
crème fraîche
chocolate-dipped fruits
cocoa powder, to dust

1 Break the chocolate into pieces. Place the chocolate and butter in a bowl over a pan of gently simmering water and stir until melted and well combined. Remove from the heat and leave to cool.

2 Place the egg yolks in a mixing bowl with the sugar and whisk until pale and fluffy. Using an electric whisk running on low speed, slowly whisk in the cool chocolate mixture. Stir in the chocolate flavouring (extract) or chocolate-flavoured liqueur.

3 Whip the cream until just holding its shape. Fold into the chocolate mixture. Spoon into 6 small ramekins (custard pots), or individual metal moulds (molds). Leave to chill for at least 2 hours.

4 To serve, turn out the desserts on to individual serving dishes. If you have difficulty turning them out, dip the moulds (molds) into a bowl of warm water for a few seconds to help the marquise to slip out. Serve with chocolate-dipped fruit and crème fraîche and dust with cocoa powder.

COOK'S TIP

The slight tartness of the crème fraîche contrasts well with this very rich dessert. Dip the fruit in white chocolate to give a good colour contrast.

Rich Chocolate Ice Cream

A rich flavoured chocolate ice cream which is delicious served on its own or with a chocolate sauce. For a special dessert, serve in these attractive trellis cups.

Serves 6-8

INGREDIENTS

ICE CREAM:
1 egg
3 egg yolks
90 g/3 oz/6 tbsp caster (superfine) sugar

300 ml/¹/₂ pint/1¹/₄ cups full cream milk
250 g/9 oz dark chocolate
300 ml/¹/₂ pint/1¹/₄ cups double (heavy) cream

TRELLIS CUPS:
100 g/3¹/₂ oz dark chocolate

1 Beat together the egg, egg yolks and caster (superfine) sugar in a mixing bowl until well combined. Heat the milk until almost boiling.

2 Gradually pour the hot milk on to the eggs, whisking as you do so. Place the bowl over a pan of gently simmering water and cook, stirring until the mixture thickens sufficiently to thinly coat the back of a wooden spoon.

3 Break the dark chocolate into small pieces and add to the hot custard. Stir until the chocolate has melted. Cover with a sheet of dampened baking parchment and leave to cool.

4 Whip the cream until just holding its shape, then fold into the cooled chocolate custard. Transfer to a freezer container and freeze for 1-2 hours until the mixture is frozen 2.5 cm/1 inch from the sides.

5 Scrape the ice cream into a chilled bowl and beat again until smooth. Re-freeze until firm.

6 To make the trellis cups, invert a muffin tray (pan) and cover 6 alternate mounds with cling film (plastic wrap). Melt the chocolate, place it in a paper piping bag and snip off the end.

7 Pipe a circle around the base of the mound, then pipe chocolate back and forth over it to form a trellis; carefully pipe a double thickness. Pipe around the base again. Chill until set, then lift from the tray (pan) and remove the cling film (plastic wrap). Serve the ice cream in the trellis cups.

Marble Cheesecake

*A dark and white chocolate cheesecake filling is marbled together
to a give an attractive finish to this rich and decadent dessert.*

Serves 10–12

INGREDIENTS

BASE:
225 g/8 oz toasted oat cereal
50 g/1³/4 oz/¹/2 cup toasted
　hazelnuts, chopped
50 g/1³/4 oz/4 tbsp butter
25 g/1 oz dark chocolate

FILLING:
350 g/12 oz full fat soft cheese
100 g/3¹/2 oz/7 tbsp caster
　(superfine) sugar
200 ml/7 fl oz/³/4 cup thick yogurt

300 ml/¹/2 pint/1¹/4 cups double
　(heavy) cream
1 sachet (envelope) gelatine
3 tbsp water
175 g/6 oz dark chocolate, melted
175 g/6 oz white chocolate, melted

1 Place the toasted oat cereal in a plastic bag and crush with a rolling pin. Pour the crushed cereal into a mixing bowl and stir in the hazelnuts.

2 Melt the butter and chocolate together over a low heat and stir into the cereal mixture, stirring until well coated.

3 Using the bottom of a glass, press the mixture into the base and up the sides of a 20 cm/ 8 inch springform tin (pan).

4 Beat together the cheese and sugar with a wooden spoon until smooth. Beat in the yogurt. Whip the cream until just holding its shape and fold into the mixture. Sprinkle the gelatine over the water in a heatproof bowl and leave to go spongy. Place over a pan of hot water and stir until dissolved. Stir into the mixture.

5 Divide the mixture in half and beat the dark chocolate into one half and the white chocolate into the other half.

6 Place alternate spoonfuls of mixture on top of the cereal base. Swirl the filling together with the tip of a knife to give a marbled effect. Level the top with a scraper or a palette knife (spatula). Leave to chill until set before serving.

COOK'S TIP

For a lighter texture, fold in 2 egg whites whipped to soft peaks before folding in the cream in step 4.

Chocolate Brandy Torte

A crumbly ginger chocolate base, topped with velvety smooth chocolate brandy cream makes this a blissful cake.

Serves 12

INGREDIENTS

BASE:
250 g/9 oz gingernut biscuits
75 g/2³/4 oz dark chocolate
100 g/3¹/2 oz/generous ¹/3 cup butter

FILLING:
225 g/8 oz dark chocolate

250 g/9 oz mascarpone cheese
2 eggs, separated
3 tbsp brandy
300 ml/¹/2 pint/1¹/4 cups double (heavy) cream
50 g/1³/4 oz/4 tbsp caster (superfine) sugar

TO DECORATE:
100 ml/3¹/2 fl oz/scant ¹/2 cup double (heavy) cream
chocolate coffee beans

1 Crush the biscuits in a bag with a rolling pin or in a food processor. Melt the chocolate and butter together and pour over the biscuits. Mix well, then use to line the base and sides of a 23 cm/ 9 inch loose-bottomed fluted flan tin (pan) or springform tin (pan). Leave to chill whilst preparing the filling.

2 To make the filling, melt the dark chocolate in a pan, remove from the heat and beat in the mascarpone cheese, egg yolks and brandy.

3 Lightly whip the cream until just holding its shape and fold in the chocolate mixture.

4 Whisk the egg whites in a grease-free bowl until standing in soft peaks. Add the caster (superfine) sugar a little at a time and whisk until thick and glossy. Fold into the chocolate mixture, in 2 batches, until just mixed.

5 Spoon the mixture into the prepared base and chill for at least 2 hours. Carefully transfer to a serving plate. To decorate, whip the cream and pipe on to the cheesecake and add the chocolate coffee beans.

VARIATION

If chocolate coffee beans are unavailable, use chocolate-coated raisins to decorate.

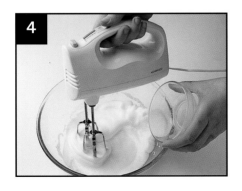

Chocolate Freezer Cake

Hidden in a ring of chocolate cake lies the secret to this freezer cake, a chocolate and mint ice cream. You can use orange or coffee ice cream if preferred.

Serves 8–10

INGREDIENTS

4 eggs
175 g/6 oz/³/₄ cup caster (superfine) sugar

100 g/3¹/₂ oz/³/₄ cup self-raising flour
40 g/1¹/₂ oz/3 tbsp cocoa powder

500 ml/¹/₂ litre/2¹/₄ cups chocolate and mint ice cream
Chocolate Sauce

1 Lightly grease a 23 cm/9 inch ring tin (pan). Place the eggs and sugar in a large mixing bowl. Using an electric whisk if you have one, whisk the mixture until it is very thick and the whisk leaves a trail. If using a balloon whisk, stand the bowl over a pan of hot water whilst whisking.

2 Sieve (strain) the flour and cocoa together and fold into the egg mixture. Pour into the prepared tin (pan) and bake in a preheated oven, 180°C/350°F/Gas Mark 4, for 30 minutes or until springy to the touch. Leave to cool in the tin (pan) before turning out on to a wire rack to cool completely.

3 Rinse the cake tin (pan) and line with a strip of cling film (plastic wrap), overhanging slightly. Cut the top off the cake about 1 cm/¹/₂ inch thick and set aside.

4 Return the cake to the tin (pan). Using a spoon, scoop out the centre of the cake leaving a shell about 1 cm/¹/₂ inch thick.

5 Remove the ice cream from the freezer and leave to stand for a few minutes, then beat with a wooden spoon until softened a little. Fill the centre of the cake with the ice cream, levelling the top. Replace the top of the cake.

6 Cover with the overhanging cling film (plastic wrap) and freeze for at least 2 hours.

7 To serve, turn the cake out on to a serving dish and drizzle over some of the chocolate sauce in an attractive pattern, if you wish. Cut the cake into slices and serve the remaining sauce separately.

Easy Chocolate Fudge

This is the easiest fudge to make – for a really rich flavour, use a good dark chocolate with a high cocoa content, ideally at least 70 per cent.

Makes 25–30 pieces

INGREDIENTS

500 g/1 lb 2 oz dark chocolate
75 g/2^3/$_4$ oz/^{1}/$_3$ cup unsalted butter

400 g/14 oz can sweetened
condensed milk

^{1}/$_2$ tsp vanilla flavouring (extract)

1 Lightly grease a 20 cm/8 inch square cake tin (pan).

2 Break the chocolate into pieces and place in a large saucepan with the butter and condensed milk.

3 Heat gently, stirring until the chocolate and butter melts and the mixture is smooth. Do not allow to boil.

4 Remove from the heat. Beat in the vanilla flavouring (extract), then beat the mixture for a few minutes until thickened. Pour it into the prepared tin (pan) and level the top.

5 Chill the mixture in the refrigerator until firm.

6 Tip the fudge out on to a chopping board and cut into squares to serve.

VARIATION

For chocolate peanut fudge, replace 50 g/1^1/$_2$ oz/4 tbsp of the butter with crunchy peanut butter.

COOK'S TIP

Don't use milk chocolate as the results will be too sticky.

COOK'S TIP

Store the fudge in an airtight container in a cool, dry place for up to 1 month. Do not freeze.

This is a Parragon Book
First published in 2003

Parragon
Queen Street House
4 Queen Street, Bath, BA1 1HE, UK

Copyright © Parragon 2003

All recipes and photography compiled from material
created by 'Haldane Mason', and 'The Foundry'.

Cover design by Shelley Doyle.

ISBN: 1-40540-822-7

Printed in China

NOTE

This book uses imperial and metric measurements. Follow the same units
of measurement throughout; do not mix imperial and metric. All spoon
measurements are level; teaspoons are assumed to be 5 ml and
tablespoons are assumed to be 15 ml. Unless otherwise stated, milk is
assumed to be whole milk, eggs and individual vegetables such as
potatoes are medium, and pepper is freshly ground black pepper.

The times given for each recipe are an approximate guide only because
the preparation times may differ according to the techniques used by
different people and the cooking times may vary as a result of the type of
oven used.

Recipes using raw or very lightly cooked eggs should be avoided by
infants, the elderly, pregnant women, convalescents and anyone suffering
from an illness.